Post Card

FOREIGN LANGUAGES PRESS · 外 文 出 版 社

Crested ibis

RARE WILD ANIMALS

First Edition 2002

Rare Wild Animals

ISBN 7-119-03060-4

© Foreign Languages Press
Published by Foreign Languages Press
24 Baiwanzhuang Road, Beijing 100037, China
Home Page: http://www.flp.com.cn
E-mail Addresses: info@flp.com.cn
                  sales@flp.com.cn
Distributed by China International Book Trading Corporation
35 Chegongzhuang Xilu, Beijing 100044, China
P.O.Box 399, Beijing ,China

Printed in the People's Republic of China

RARE WILD ANIMALS

by Zhang Cizu

Foreign Languages Press Beijing

Contents

PREFACE

The human race achieved remarkable success in "conquering nature" during the 20th century. But, nature also hit back to punish human presumption. The decline of forestry coverage, deterioration of grassland, drought in wetlands and air pollution not only brought great trouble to humans, but also decimated wildlife. In the early 1990s, Birdlife International reported that at least 1,000 of the 9,000 recognized species of birds had either disappeared, or were on the verge of extinction. Now, more and more people realize that nature plays an important role in the development of society, and we should seek to live harmoniously with nature rather than trying to conquer it.

With its vast area, diverse landscape and climate variations, China harbors a rich variety of wildlife. It is one of ten countries with the largest numbers of biological species in the world. In terms of temperature, the

nation can be divided from south to north into equatorial, tropical, subtropical, warm-temperate, temperate and cold-temperate zones. In terms of moisture, it can also be divided from southeast to northwest into humid, semi-humid, semi-arid and arid zones. China's topography is varied and complicated, with towering mountains, different sized basins, undulating plateaus and fertile plains. The change of climate and altitude naturally produce many differences in the types of wildlife prevalent in each area. The wildlife typical of mountains, deserts and prairies are mainly spread north of the Qinling and Hengduan Mountain Ranges, while tropical and subtropical animals live to the south of these ranges. But, in the transitional areas between different types of climate or topography, there may be some overlap as some species expand their living areas beyond traditional boundaries. For example, tropical and subtropical animals such as Rhesus Macaque and Masked Civet can also be found in northern China. The wolf and fox have moved out of their traditional habitat in the north into the rest of the country. Located in western China, the Tibetan Plateau and Mongolian Plateau are very cold and arid, and can only support Yaks, Tibetan Antelopes, Mongolian Gazelles, Marmots and other wildlife capable of adapting to such a harsh environment.

China has over 4,640 vertebrate species, including 450 mammals, 1,329 birds, 387 reptiles, 274 amphibians and over 2,200 fishes, accounting for ten percent of all the world's vertebrate species. Among them, more than one hundred species such as the Giant Panda, Chinese River Dolphin, Golden Monkey, White-lipped Deer, Brown-eared Pheasant, Golden Pheasant, Black-necked Crane, Chinese Giant Salamander, Chinese Alligator and Chinese Crocodilian Lizard are native to China. The Giant Panda, a world-renowned wildlife species, can only live in a natural state in the western mountainous areas of Sichuan Province, the Min Mountain and on the southern slope of the Qinling Mountain Range. Of the 15

species of cranes in the world, nine are found in China. Additionally, China has 61 of the world's total of 281 pheasant species. More than 20 species of pheasants are either unique to, or mainly live in China.

Owing to excessive exploitation of nature, rapid population increase and the development of industries, wildlife is suffering a catastrophic decline and more than ten species of animals, including the Wild Horse and David's Deer have been extinct in the wild. Nearly one hundred animals including the Giant Panda, Tiger, Asiatic Elephant and Crested Ibis are listed as endangered species. Poaching makes the situation even worse, so that wildlife protection has become an increasingly important issue.

Since the founding of New China in 1949, the government has promulgated a series of regulations, and finally established its first law for protecting wildlife – "Wildlife Protection Law of the People's Republic of

China" – in November 1988. Some other laws and policies were issued by both central and local governments in the ensuing years, laying a solid legal foundation for the protection of wildlife.

China has made remarkable achievements in protecting and breeding rare and endangered species. Since the 1980s, for example, the Ministry of Forestry has been cooperating with the World Wide Fund for Nature (formerly the World Wildlife Foundation) on the study and protection of the Giant Panda. Only seven Crested Ibises were found in northern China's Shaanxi Province in 1981, when a Crested Ibis Conservation Area was set up. Now, the number has increased to nearly 300. After nearly 20 years of hard work, the Xuanzhou Chinese

Alligator Breeding and Research Center in Anhui Province has managed to increase the number of Chinese Alligators from less than 500 to more than ten thousand.

The Chinese government has paid great attention to natural reserve construction as a means of protecting wildlife. So far, more than 1,000 sites covering 120 million hectares, approximately 12 percent of Chinese territory, have been declared as natural reserves. Some endangered species have begun a gradual recovery and steady population growth.

The cause of wildlife conservation in China has attracted international concern and support, and the government has signed a number of international treaties on the protection of wildlife and nature in general. It has also signed agreements with foreign countries on the protection of migratory birds, the Giant Panda and the Tiger. Scientific exchanges between Chinese and international conservation organizations are quite frequent.

Wildlife is a treasure of mankind and an important part of the natural environment. They are our close friends, not our enemies. We have the responsibility and obligation to preserve valuable wildlife for coming generations.

MAMMALS

China has some 450 mammal species. More than 90 species, including the Giant Panda, Golden Monkey, Chinese River Dolphin, Takin and Asiatic Elephant, have been listed as national key-protected wildlife and are under close State protection. The government has imported some species, such as David's Deer and Wild Horse, which had become extinct in the wild in China, from foreign countries for breeding purposes. Many nature reserves have also been established to protect valuable mammals.

Pig-tailed Macaque

Macaca nemestrina

Primates Cercopithecidae

Distribution: southern areas of China's Yunnan Province, India, Myanmar, Thailand, Malaysia and Sumatra

The body length of Pig-tailed Macaque is about 60 cm with a tail 15-18cm long. They weigh 11-14kg and live in dense forest under the lead of a "king". Fruits are their main food, but they also eat insects, worms and birds' eggs. The normal lifespan is about 25 years. The males are ferocious.

They are listed as first grade nationally protected animals.

Hoolock Gibbon; White Browed Gibbon

Hylobates hoolock

Primates Hylobatidae

Distribution: Mt Gaoligong in southwestern China's Yunnan Province, Myanmar, Bangladesh and India

The body length of the Hoolock Gibbon is in the range of 44.5-58cm and it weighs 7-8kg. The males are black and brown, while the females are yellow and brown. Their white eyebrows are the most notable feature. Hoolock Gibbons live in small groups on trees in tropical primitive forests almost all year around. Their staple foods are mature fruits and tender leaves. They also feed on insects, birds' eggs and fledglings.The Hoolock Gibbon can live 20-25 years.

They are listed as first grade nationally protected animals.

next tree. They can leap distances of more than 5 meters. The White Handed Gibbons move and live in families. Branches, tender leaves flowers, fruits are their main food, but sometimes they also eat insects The normal lifespan is about 32 years.

They are listed as the first grade nationally protected animals.

White Handed Gibbon; Common Gibbon; Lar Gibbon
Hylobates lar
Primates Hylobatidae
Distribution: southwestern areas of China's Yunnan Province, Southeast Asia

The body length of the White Handed Gibbon is 37-50 cm and it weighs 4-5kg. They have long arms and often yell. White Handed Gibbons live in tropical forests, and swing through the trees using their long arms like pendulums until they work up enough momentum to reach the

Rhesus Macaque

Macaca mulatta

Primates Cercopithecidae

Distribution: southern China, India, Nepal and Afghanistan

    The body length of the Rhesus Macaque is 51-60cm, with a tail 20-32 cm long; they weigh 3-6kg. They can survive in various environments. As gregarious animals, they often live in groups under the leadership of a king. They are omnivorous. The normal lifespan is 25-30 years.

    They are listed as second grade nationally protected animals.

Yunnan Snub-nose Monkey

Rhinopithecus bieti

Primates Cercopithecidae

Distribution: northwestern areas of China's Yunnan Province, southeast Tibet

The body length of the Yunnan Snub-nose Monkey 74-83cm, with a tail shorter than the body. Males weig more than 20 kg. They are the primates that are able to liv at the highest altitude in the world. They often live in f forests along the Yunnan-Tibet border more than 3,00 meters above sea level. The Yunnan Snub-nose Monkey gregarious and the number of each group varies from 5 200.

They are listed as first grade nationally protecte animals.

Francois' Monkey

Presbytis francoisi

Primates Cercopithecidae

Distribution: southern areas of China's Guangxi Zhuang Autonomous Region, northern Vietnam, western and central areas of Laos

The body length of Francois' Monkey is 50-60cm, with a tail 79-86cm long. They live in tropical and sub-tropical forests and sometimes they also dwell in hilly areas. Under the leadership of a male monkey, they search for food, including leaves, buds, fruits, insects and small animals, among trees in small groups. They sleep on trees or in caves.The normal lifespan is about 12 years.

They are listed as first grade nationally protected animals.

White-headed Leaf-monkey
Presbytis leucocephalus
Primates Cercopithecidae
Distribution: southern area of China's Guangxi Zhuang
Autonomous Region

The body length of the White-headed Leaf-monkey i
52-71cm, with a tail 70-90cm long. They weigh 6-9.5kg
and live in tropical and sub-tropical forests. They are good
climbers. Living in small groups, they move within fixed
routes and have a stable habitat in caves and stone crevices
The normal lifespan is about 12 years.

They are listed as first grade nationally protected
animals.

Golden Monkey
Rhinopithecus roxellanae
Primates Cercopithecidae
Distribution: Sichuan, Shaanxi, Gansu and Hubei provinces

The body length of the Golden Monkey is 53-77cm and the tail is almost as long as the bodies. The females are smaller than the males and are of a lighter color. The Golden Monkey lives in forests at an altitude of 1,500-3,000 meters. The Golden Monkey is gregarious and the number in each group varies from several dozen to more than a hundred. Under the leadership of the strongest male, they live in trees and can endure bitter cold. The normal lifespan is 16-18 years.

They are exclusively found in China and listed as first grade nationally protected animals.

Slow Loris

Nycticebus coucang

Primates Lorisidae

Distribution: southern areas of China's Yunnan and Guangxi Zhuang Autonomous Region, Southeast Asia to Indonesia

The body lengths of the Slow Loris is 26-38cm, with 1-2cm tail; they weigh 1-2kg. Their habitats are primitive forests in tropical and sub-tropical areas. Living on trees they are nocturnal animals that move slowly. They feed on wild fruits and insects, but also eat fledglings and birds eggs. The Slow Loris is a solitary animal and lives with others only during the mating season. The normal lifespan is 12-14 years.

They are listed as first grade nationally protected animals in China.

Sun Bear

Helarctos malayanus

Carnivora Ursidea

Distribution: China's Guangdong Province, Guangxi Zhuang Autonomous Region and Yunnan Province, South Asia and Southeast Asia

The body length of the Sun Bears is 100-140cm, with a 3-7cm tail. They weigh 27-65kg and they are the smallest bears. Living in dense forests, they are good at climbing trees. They don't hibernate in winter and move nimbly. They are solitary animals. The normal lifespan is about 24 years.

As rare animals in China, they are given first grade national protection.

Brown Bear; Grizzly Bear

Ursus arctos

Carnivora Ursidea

Distribution: northeastern China, Tibetan Plateau, northern Asia-Europe Continent and North America

The body length of the Brown Bear is 170-210cm, with a 6-21cm tail; weight can vary from 140 to 450kg. They dwell in forests or plains. They are not good at climbing up trees and they are solitary animals. They have sharp sense of hearing and smell, but their eyesight is poor. They mainly feed on plants and hibernate in winter. The normal lifespan is more than 30 years.

They are listed as second grade nationally protected animals.

Asiatic Black Bear

Selenarctos thibetanus

Carnivora Ursidea

Distribution: northern and southern China, Japan, Korea, South Asia and Southeast Asia

The body length of the Asiatic Black Bear is 120-180cm, with a 6.5-16cm tail. The males weigh 110-250kg and the females weigh 65-125kg.

They are solitary animals living in broad-leaf forests or mixed forests. Good climbers and swimmers, they also have a sharp sense of hearing and smell, but their eyesight is poor and so they are also called "Blind Bears". The normal lifespan is about 30 years. Asiatic Black Bears living in northern areas hibernate in winter.

They are listed as second grade nationally protected animals in China.

Chinese Pangolin

Manis Pentadactyla

Pholidota Manidae

Distribution: southern China, Myanmar, Nepal, Sikkim, Thailand

    The body length of the Chinese Pangolin is about 100cm. They live in wet forest areas in hills or plains. They are nocturnal animals and live alone or in pairs. They are able to climb trees and swim. The Chinese Pangolin often twists its body into the shape of a ball when encountering enemies. Being good diggers, they live in holes. Babies are carried on the mother's back when walking. The normal lifespan is about 1 years.

    They are listed as second grade nationally protected animals.

Chinese River Dolphin

Lipotes vexillifer

Cetacea Platanistidae

Distribution: middle and lower reaches of the Yangtze River

The body length of the Chinese River Dolphins is 1.5-2.5m and it weighs 100-200kg. They move alone or in small groups of two to seven. They come to the surface to breathe every 10-20 seconds and live on fish weighing less than 1,000g.

There are only about 100 Chinese River Dolphins. Exclusively found in China, they are listed as first grade nationally protected animals.

Dhole; Asiatic Wild Dog; Red Dog
Cuon alpinus
Carnivora Canidae
Distribution: southern China and southern Tibet, Middl‹
Asia to Southeast Asia

　　The body length of the Dhole is 88-113cm, with
40-50cm tail; they weigh 10-21kg. They dwell in caves o
hilly areas, dense forests, and mountainous areas. They ar‹
gregarious animals and feed on other mammals. They als‹
eat insects and rotten flesh.The lifespan is 15-16 years.

　　They receive second grade national protection.

Binturong

Arctictis binturong

Carnivora Viverridae

Distribution: southern areas of China's Yunnan Province, Southeast Asia

The body length of the Binturong is 61-96cm, with a 56-89cm tail; weight varies from 9 to 14kg. They dwell in the trees of dense forests. They are nocturnal animals and move alone or in small groups. They are able to dive, swim and catch fish. The normal lifespan is 22 years.

The Binturongs are listed as first grade nationally protected animals in China.

South China Tiger

Panthera tigris amoyensis

Carnivora Felidae

Distribution: China's southeastern, eastern, southern and southwestern areas

The body length of the South China Tiger is 140-280cm, with a 60-95cm tail. The males weigh 149-225kg and females 90-120kg. They live alone in forests, jungles and dense wild grass. They are ferocious animals. The normal lifespan is about 20 years.

They are listed as first grade nationally protected animals.

Siberian Tiger

Panthera tigris altaica

Carnivora Felidae

Distribution: Lesser Hingger Mountains and Changbai Mountain; Siberia and Korea

The body length of the Siberian Tiger is 140-280cm, with a 60-90cm tail. The males weigh 180-306kg and females 100-167kg. They are the largest species of the cat family. They live alone in forests, jungles and dense wild grass. They are nocturnal animals and excel in swimming. Big mammals are their usual prey. The normal lifespan varies from 20 to 25 years.

They are listed as first grade nationally protected animals.

Clouded Leopard

Neofelis nebulosa

Carnivora Felidae

Distribution: China's southeastern and southwestern areas, Nepal, Malaysia, Sumatra

The body length of the Clouded Leopard is 61-106cm, with 55-91cm tail; the weight ranges from 16 to 32kg. They dwell in the trees of tropical and subtropical forests. Being solitary and nocturnal animals, they have sharp hearing, good eyesight and a strong sense of smell and they excel in climbing and leaping. They live by catching birds, monkeys, boars, deer, goats and rabbits.The normal lifespan is 15-17 years.

They are listed as second grade nationally protected animals.

Snow Leopard

Panthera uncia

Carnivora Felidae

Distribution: China's southwestern and northwestern areas, Afghanistan
o Lake Baikal

The body length of the Snow Leopard is 110-130cm, with a 80-90cm

tail. They weigh 38-75kg. They dwell in rocky areas of n...
altitude of 2,700-6,000 meters. They are solitary animals and ...
for blue sheep, argali, deer, boars, marmots, mice and rabbits ...
daytime. The normal lifespan is about 20 years.

They are listed as first grade nationally protected animals.

Pallas's Cat
Felis manul
Carnivora Felidae
Distribution: China's northeastern, northern and northwestern areas
Caspian Sea borders and Iran to southeastern Siberia.

The body length of the Pallas's Cat is 50-65cm, with 21-35cm tail
the weight ranges from 2.3 to 3.5kg. They live alone in the desert and
rocky areas at an altitude of 4,000 meters. They are nocturnal animals
and move nimbly. They feed on small mammals. The normal lifespan
ranges from 10 to 15 years.

They receive second grade national protection.

Wild Horse

Equus przewalskii

Perissodactyla Equidae

Distribution: originally in the northeastern areas of China's Xinjiang Uygur Autonomous Region to Inner Mongolia and Mongolia

The body length of the Wild Horse is 220-280cm, with a 92-110cm tail; weight averages 350kg. They live in deserts, prairie, hilly areas, Gobi land and wet grasslands in small groups. Being good runners, they also like bathing in the sand and swimming. Grass and wild vegetables are their main food. The normal lifespan ranges from 25-35 years.

They are listed as first grade nationally protected animals.

Asiatic Elephant; Indian Elephant

Elephas maximus

Proboscidea Elephantidae

Distribution: southern areas of China's Yunnan Province, South Asia and Southeast Asia

The body length of the Asiatic Elephant is 550-640cm with a 120-150cm tail.Weighing 5,000kg, they are the largest mammals living on the continent and only the males have ivories. The Asiatic Elephant lives in tropical and subtropical forests, jungles and grasslands. Each group consists of several up to several dozen elephants. They like water and can stay in the rivers or ponds for several hours when it is hot. They feed on grass, leaves, bamboo leaves and wild fruits. The normal lifespan ranges from 70 to 80 years. Their trunks are so nimble that they can pick up needles and remove a screw.

They receive first grade national protection.

...tan Plateau

...he Kiang is 200-220cm, with a 43-49cm tail; ...o 270kg. They live in the Gobi Desert and hilly areas of the Tibetan Plateau. They are gregarious animals and excel at running. In the daytime, they roam on the grasslands to search for grass and wild vegetables. The normal lifespan ranges from 25 to 30 years.

Native to China, they are listed as first grade nationally protected animals.

Gaur; Indian Bison

Bos gaurus

Artiodactyla Bovidae

Distribution: southern part of China's Yunnan Province, southeastern Tibet, India to Indochina Peninsula and Malaysian Peninsula

The body length of the Gaur is 230-250cm, with a 70-105cm tail; weight ranges from 650-1000kg. They live in grasslands and forests from sea level to an altitude of 1,800 meters. They roam in small groups of eight to 11. Gaurs are ferocious and feed on grass and leaves. The normal lifespan ranges from 20 to 30 years.

They receive first grade national protection.

Yak

Bos grunniens

Artiodactyla Bovidae

Distribution: Tibetan Plateau

Weighing 821kg, the male yak is 203cm high from its heel to shoulder and its horn is 80 meters long. Weighing 306kg, the female yak is 156cm high from its heel to shoulder and its horn is 51cm long. They dwell in the mountainous grasslands and cold deserts at an altitude of 4,000-6,100 meters. Dozens of females and cubs form a group and live together. The adult males live alone or in small groups, each of which is made up of only two or three beasts. They can eat all of plants, but Greminaceous grass is their favorite food. The normal lifespan is 25 years.

They are native to China and are listed as the country's first grade nationally protected animals.

David's Deer
Elaphurus davidianus
Artiodactyla Cervidae
Distribution: originally in eastern China's coastal plains

The body length of the David's Deer is about 150cm, with a 50cm tail. Weighing 150-200kg, their appearance is quite spectacular. Their tails are similar to that of the horse; their hooves are similar to those of the cow; their antlers are similar to a deer's, and their body is similar to a donkey. Hence, they are also called "nondescript animals". They gregariously search for grass and water plants. The normal lifespan is about 20 years.

They are listed as the first grade nationally protected animals.

Thorold's Deer; White-lipped Deer

Cervus albirostris

Artiodactyla Cervidae

Distribution: Tibetan Plateau

The body length of the Thorold's Deer is 210cm, with a 10-13cm tail. Weighing 250kg, they dwell in mountainous grasslands at an altitude of 3,500-5,200 meters. Thorold's Deer is able to climb sand hills and steep cliffs and they are the members of the deer family living at the highest altitude. Being gregarious animals, they feed on Greminaceous grass. The normal lifespan is about 20 years.

They are listed as first grade nationally protected animals.

Sika Deer

Cervus nippon

Artiodactyla Cervidae

Distribution: border areas of China's Jiangxi, Anhui and Zhejiang provinces, Japan, Korea and Vietnam

The body length of the Sika Deer is 150-170cm, with a 13-18cm tail; weight ranges from 40-150kg. They gregariously dwell in the mountainous grasslands and forest margins. They feed on green grass and leaves and often lick saline soil. The normal lifespan is 20 years.

They receive first grade national protection.

Tufted Deer

Elaphodus cephalophus

Artiodactyla Cervidae

Distribution: China's Qinling Mountain Range and area south of the Yangtze River

The body length of the Tufted Deer is 82-119cm, with a 8-13cm tail; weight ranges from 15 to 28kg. They dwell in the subtropical mountainous forests in pairs. They feed on grass and tender tree twigs. Mushrooms and fruits are their favorite food. The males have sharp canines. The normal lifespan is nine years.

They are native to China and listed as second grade nationally protected animals.

Black Muntjac

Muntiacus crinifrons

Artiodactyla Cervidae

Distribution: western areas of Zhejiang Province, southern Anhui Province and surrounding areas

The body length of the Black Muntjac is 98-113cm,
with a 18-24cm tail; weight ranges from 21 to 28.5kg. They
live in subtropical, broad-leaf forests in mountainous areas at an altitude of 1,000 meters or more. They feed mainly
on bushes and tender twigs, but grass, fern, mushroom and
fruits are also consumed. The normal lifespan is 10-11 years.

They receive first grade national protection.

Chinese Water Deer

Hydropotes inermis

Artiodactyla Cervidae

Distribution: coastal areas or riverside of southeastern Chir

The body length of Chinese Water Deer is 91-103cm with 6-7cm tail; weight ranges from 14 to 17kg. The male upper canines are very sharp. They live on the banks (rivers, lakes, reed marshes and grassy lands. Movin quickly alone or in pairs, they like water and can swim Reeds and coarse grass are their favorite food and the breeding skills are the best among deer.The normal lifespa is 10-12 years.

They receive second grade national protection.

Lesser Malay Chevrotain

Tragulus javanicus

Artiodactyla Tragulidae

Distribution: southern areas of Yunnan Province,Indochina Peninsula to Kalimantan

The body length of the Lesser Malay Chevrotains is 42-48cm, with a 5-8cm tail. They weigh 1.2-2.5kg and have no horns. The males have sharp upper canines. Being nocturnal animals, they live alone in tropical jungles and feed on tender twigs, leaves and wild fruits. The normal lifespan is 14 years.

They are listed as first grade nationally protected animals.

Bharal; Blue Sheep
Pseudois nayaur
Artiodactyla Bovidae
Distribution: China's northwestern and southwestern areas,
Kashmir and Nepal

The body length of the Bharal is 108-140cm, with a
3-20cm tail; weight ranges from 45 to 74kg. They live
gregariously in the rocky grasslands of mountains and val-
eys at an altitude of 3,000-6,000 meters, living off
reminaceous plants, grass and lichen. The normal lifespan
s 24 years.

They are listed as second grade nationally protected
nimals in China.

Himalayan Tahr

Hemitragus jemlahicus

Artiodactyla Bovidae

Distribution: southern Tibet, Kashmir, India and Nepal

The body length of the Himalayan Tahr is 130-170cm, with a 9cm tail. The males weigh about 108kg. Dwelling in rugged, forested hills a an altitude of 3,000-4,000 meters, they live in groups of between tw and 20. Greminaceous plants and nut grass flat sedge are their stapl food. The normal lifespan is about 21 years.

They are listed as first grade nationally protected animals in China

Takin

Budorcas taxicolor bedfordi

Artiodactyla Bovidae

Distribution: Qinling Mountain Range in Shaanxi Province

The body length of the Takin is 170-220cm, with a 10-15cm tail. Weighing 300-600kg, they live gregariously in the mixed forests of broad-leaf trees and conifers or coniferous forests on mountains at an altitude of 2,200-2,800 meters. Twigs, sprouts, barks, bamboo leaves and grass are their main food, and they like to lick salt. The normal lifespan is 15-20 years.

Native to China, the Takins receive first grade national protection.

Red Goral

Naemorhedus cranbrooki

Artiodactyla Bovidae

Distribution: southeastern areas of Tibet and southwestern areas of China's Yunnan Province, northern Myanmar and India's Assam

The body length of the Red Goral is 93-103cm, with a 10-12cm tail. Weighing 20-30kg, they live in mountain forests and steep rocky hills at an altitude of 2,000-4,500 meters. Grass, lichen, beard moss and tender jungle leaves are their favorite food. They are good jumpers and excel in walking on steep cliffs. The normal lifespan is about 15 years.

Red Gorals are rare and receive first grade national protection.

Takin

Budorcas taxicolor tibetana

Artiodactyla Bovidae

Distribution: western areas of Sichuan Province and southeastern areas of Gansu Province

The body length of the Takin is 170-222cm, with a 10-15cm tail. Weighing 300-600kg, they live gregariously in mountain forests at an altitude of 1,500-4,000 meters. Twigs, sprouts, bark, bamboo leaves, grass and seeds are their main food, and they like to lick salt. The normal lifespan is 15-20 years.

Native to China, they receive first grade national protection.

Tibetan Antelope

Pantholops hodgsoni

Artiodactyla Bovidae

Distribution: Tibetan Plateau

The body length of the Tibetan Antelopes is 130-140cm, with a 10cm tail. Weighing 25-50kg, they dwell in mountainous deserts and prairies at an altitude of 4,000-5,500 meters. Grass and lichen are their staple food. They are gregarious animals and move in large groups.

Native to China, they enjoy first grade national protection.

Goitered Gazelle

Gazella subgutturosa

Artiodactyla Bovidae

Distribution: northern China, Palestine and Arabian Peninsula

The body length of the Goitered Gazelle is 88-109cm, with a 12-18cm tail. Weighing 29-42kg, they live gregariously in the hills and deserts. They are good at running and leaping. They can also endure cold. Leaves, tender twigs and grass are their staple food. The normal lifespan is about 17 years. The male becomes goiterous during the estrus and thus the animal gets its name.

They receive second grade national protection.

Tibetan Gazelle

Procapra picticaudata

Artiodactyla Bovidae

Distribution: Tibetan Plateau and surrounding areas

The body length of the Tibetan Gazelle is 91-105cm, with a 2-10cm tail. Weighing 20-35kg, they live gregariously in mountainous grassy marshland, deserts and prairie. Each group usually consists of three to five members. They feed on herbs.

They are native to China and receive second grade national protection.

Eurasian Beaver

Castor fiber

Rodentia Castoridae

Distribution: northeastern area of China's Xinjiang Uygur Autonomous Region, Mongolia, middle and northern Europe

The body length of the Eurasian Beaver is 60-100cm, with a 21-29.5cm tail. Weighing 17-30kg, they live gregariously on the banks of rivers in holes dug by themselves. The normal lifespan is 12-20 years.

They enjoy first grade national protection.

BIRDS

Birds are capable of flying and they have the following features: stable temperature, breeding by laying eggs and hatching them, and having feathers. But there are some exceptions. For instance, the ostrich and penguin are birds, but they cannot fly. There are about 9,000 species of birds in the world and they are distributed over the various continents, rivers and seas.

China's vast land, complicated topography and various climates have produced a wide variety of species. Up to now, 1,329 species have been found living in China, accounting for more than 14 % of the birds in the world.

Crested Ibis

Nipponia nippon

Ciconiiformes Threskiornithidae

Distribution: Yang County in China's Shaanxi Province

    The Crested Ibis is 55cm long and it is on the verge of extinction. They usually move around the shallow water and perch on high trees. When flying, they move their wings slowly, but strongly. The Crested Ibis is a very rare and beautiful bird.

    They are native to China and receive first grade national protection.

Rosy Pelican

Pelecanus onocrotalus

Pelecaniformes Pelecanidae

Distribution: China's Xinjiang Uygur Autonomous Region and Qinghai Province, southwestern Asia, southern Europe and northern Africa

Rosy Pelicans are 160cm long. They are quiet, large waterfowls slow in action. The gregarious Rosy Pelicans often dwell in the delta areas and wide river valleys. Their eyesight is excellent and they live by catching fish.

They receive second grade national protection in China.

Spot-billed Pelican

Pelecanus philippensis

Pelecaniformes Pelecanidae

Distribution: lakes and coastal areas to the south of China's Shandong Province, broad expanses of water in Europe, Asia and Africa

The Spot-billed Pelicans are 140cm long. They fly around coastal areas, rivers and lakes in groups. They also excel in swimming. When fishing, they form a line or half a circle in the water and then drive fish from deep water into shallow sand.

They receive second grade national protection in China.

Mute Swan
Cygnus olor
Anseriformes Anatidae
Distribution: China's Qinghai Province, Xinjiang Uygur Autonomous Region, Inner Mongolia, and the Euro-Asian Continent

Mute Swans are 152cm long. They are the largest, heaviest and most beautiful type of swans. Dwelling in rivers and lakes, they energetically search the water for food, but are slow movers on land. Couples live together all their lives. During the breeding period, they strongly object to outsiders entering their territory. Mute Swans are quiet.

They receive second grade national protection.

Whooper Swan

Cygnus cygnus

Anseriformes Anatidae

Distribution: breeds in northern Europe and Asia, migrate south in winter

Whooper Swans are 155cm long. They live in group in large marshlands and lakes with luxuriant water plan growth. A couple or several couples live together whe breeding. In winter, they migrate to the south in groups.

They receive second grade national protection.

Whistling Swan

Cygnus columbianus

Anseriformes Anatidae

Distribution: breeds in northern Europe and northern Asia, migrates to central China in winter

Whistling Swans are 142cm long. They breed in the Siberian tundra and fly through northeastern China to the lakes on the lower reaches of the Yangtze River in winter. They are more timid than Whooper Swans and easily alarmed.

They receive second grade national protection.

Mandarin Duck
Aix galericulata
Anseriformes Anatidae
Distribution: eastern China, Siberia, Korea and Japan

    The Mandarin Ducks are 40cm long. They are colorful, and the males have beautiful feathers shaped like sails. They often perch on quiet brooks, lakes with dense trees on their banks, or on the rivers near mountains. They usually move in pairs, but in winter they live in groups.Because a couple of Mandarin Ducks never separate, in Chinese literature, they are described as the symbol of pure love.

    They receive second grade national protection.

Greater White-fronted Goose

Anser albifrons

Anseriformes Anatidae

Distribution: breeds in the frozen tundra in the Northern Hemisphere, winters in temperate zones

The Greater White-fronted Geese are 64-72cm long and they weigh 2.1-4.5kg. Dwelling on grasslands, water fields and lakes, they spend most of the daytime on land and feed on plants and some insects.

They receive second grade national protection.

Black-faced Spoonbill
Platalea minor
Ciconiiformes Threskiornithidae
Distribution: eastern China, northern Vietnam and Korea

The Black-faced Spoonbill is 76cm long. They like to walk slowly in muddy ponds, lakes and reed ponds. As they are walking in small groups in the water, they move their mouths from here to there in search of food, such as small fish, shrimps, aquatic mollusks and aquatic insects.

They receive second grade national protection.

Black Stork
Ciconia nigra
Ciconiiformes Ciconiidae
Distribution: northern China, Europe, migrates to India and Africa in winter

The Black Stork is 100cm long. It often lives in forest, marshland, or near prairies and rivers. In winter, it migrates to the wide grassland with shallow water. They build up their nests on big trees in forests or in a rocky crevice of steep cliffs.

They receive first grade national protection in China.

White Stork

Ciconia boyciana

Ciconiiformes Ciconiidae

Distribution: northern China, Northeast Asia and Japan, migrates to the waters south of the Yangtze River in winter

The White Stork is 105cm long. It roams broad fields, ponds, marshland, shallow water and sands, and prairies in small groups or alone. It often perches on thick tree trunks to take a rest and lets out a clattering sound. The White Stork catches fish, frogs, insects, small reptiles and rodents.

They receive first grade national protection.

Little Bittern ▶

Ixobrychus minutus

Ciconiiformes Ardeidae

Distribution: Euro-Asian Continent, Africa, and Australia

The Little Bittern is 35cm long and dwells in marshland. It is a nocturnal and solitary bird. Fish, frogs, shrimps, mollusks and insects are its normal food.

They receive second grade national protection.

◀ **Little Curlew**

Numenius borealis

Charadriiformes Scolopacidae

Distribution: breeds in Northeast Asia, then flies over eastern China when migrating to Australia

Little Curlews are 31cm long. They gregariously migrate and fly over China's eastern coastal areas, marshlands, rivers and tidal areas. Fish, shrimps and mollusks are their favorite food.

They receive second grade national protection.

Great Bustard

Otis tarda

Gruiformes Otidae

Distribution: northern China, Europe, from Northwest Africa to the Middle East and Middle Asia

The Great Bustard is 100cm long. It dwells in broad prairies and wild fields. Sometimes it goes in and out of bushes. They fly slowly low in the sky. They are omnivorous. In spring, the males gather together at the same place and seek a partner. The females are responsible for building the nest and looking after the fledglings.

They receive first grade national protection.

White-naped Crane

Grus vipio

Gruiformes Gruidae

Distribution: breeds in northern China, winters in eastern China, Siberia, Mongolia, Korea and Japan

The White-naped Crane is 150cm long. They breed in northeastern and northwestern China's marshlands and reedy banks of lakes. In winter, they migrate to the lakes and rivers on the lower reaches of the Yangtze River. They build nests in dry protruding places. The male and female jointly hatch and look after the fledglings.

They receive second grade national protection.

Siberian White Crane
Grus Ieucogeranus
Gruiformes Gruidae
Distribution: breeds in Siberia; winters in China's Jiangxi Province

The Siberian White Crane is 135cm long. It lives in the tundra glades and marshland abundant with aquatic plants. It feeds on fish, shrimps, spiral shells and freshwater mussel. It also eats the roots and stems of plants.

They receive first grade national protection.

Hooded Crane

Grus monacha

Gruiformes Gruidae

Distribution: breeds in northeastern China and Siberia,
winters in southern Japan and eastern China

The Hooded Crane is 97cm long. It dwells on the plains
or marshland without forests, and it often moves among
reeds and bushes. It searches for food among the sparse
plants.

They receive first grade national protection.

Black-necked Crane

Grus nigricollis

Gruiformes Gruidae

Distribution: breeds in China's Tibetan Plateau; winters on China's Yunnan-Guizhou Plateau

The Black-necked Crane is 150cm long and it is the only species of the crane family living on plateaus. Living in lakes and marshlands gregariously, groups of Black-necked Cranes often mix with those of common cranes. Fish, shrimps, shellfish, insects, grass roots and seeds are their main food.

Native to China, they receive first grade national protection.

Red-crowned Crane

Grus japonensis

Gruiformes Gruidae

Distribution: breeds in northeastern China, Siberia and Japan; winters in Korea and eastern China

    Red-crowned Cranes are 150cm long. They dwell in broad marshlands on the banks of rivers and seas. Fish, shrimps, frogs, mice and insects are their main diet and they also eat seeds, tender twigs, roots and stems. After mating, the male and female stay close to each other and show affection. Red-crowned Cranes are the most popular cranes in China. Since ancient times, they have frequently been subjects of Chinese poetry, songs and paintings, so they are also called "immortal cranes".

    They receive first grade national protection.

Green Peafowl

Pavo muticus

Galliformes Phasianidae

Distribution: China's Yunnan Province, northeastern India, Southeast Asia and Java

    Green Peafowls are 110-240cm long. They usually dwell in the forest, bushes and bamboo forests below an altitude of 1,500 meters. They especially prefer to live in open areas of the forest near rivers. One male and several females form a group and search for food together. Wild fruits, grains, sprouts and seedlings are their main diet, but they also eat insects and small animals. They breed from May to August. During this period, the males raise and spread their beautiful tails.

    They receive first grade national protection.

Sclater's Monal

Lophophorus sclateri

Galliformes Phasianidae

Distribution: eastern part of China's Himalayas

Sclater's Monals are 70cm long. They are rare, living in mountainous marsh grasslands and bushes at an altitude of 3,000-4,000 meters. They live alone or in small groups. In winter, they move to lower altitudes. Having short tails, strong legs and beaks, they are good at digging out plant tubers for food. They also eat tender leaves, sprouts, seeds and insects. They seldom leave their habitat and don't like to fly. They are very noisy at night.

Sclater's Monals receive first grade national protection.

Grey Peacock Pheasant

Polyplectron bicalcaratum

Galliformes Phasianidae

Distribution: southwestern China, Southeast Asia

Grey Peacock Pheasants are 55-75cm long, and are beautiful and rare pheasants. The Grey Peacock Pheasant like to dwell in the wet low-lying land of forests in pairs and they search for food together. They can also be found in mountainous areas at an altitude of 1,800 meters. They dig up plants and insects for food.

They receive first grade national protection.

Temminck's Tragopan

Tragopan temminckii

Galliformes Phasianidae

Distribution: central China, eastern Himalayas, and northern Myanmar

The Temminck's Tragopan is 68cm long and it lives in the evergreen mountainous regions or mixed forests alone or in families. It perches on tree branches at night. When showing off, the males' laryngeal pouches become inflated and have blue and red designs. The males also erect their blue horns at the same time. Buds, tender sprouts and seeds are their main food, but they also eat insects. They are easily tamed and bred fast.

They receive second grade national protection.

White-eared Pheasant

Crossoptilon crossoptilon

Galliformes Phasianidae

Distribution: western areas of China's Sichuan Province, southeastern Qinghai Province, northeastern Tibet

White-eared Pheasants are 80cm long. They are native to China, dwelling in bushes at an altitude of 3,000-4,000 meters, where they perch on trees at night and escape higher up when alerted. Being omnivorous, they feed on tubers, thin roots and insects. They often drink water beside brooks in groups and build their nests in concavity areas among bushes.

They receive second grade national protection.

Brown-eared Pheasant

Crossoptilon mantchuricum

Galliformes Phasianidae

Distribution: China's Shanxi Province, Beijing and northwestern Hebei Province

Brown-eared Pheasants are 100cm long. They usually dwell in forests in lower altitude and move to higher places when being alerted. At night, they perch on trees. Tubers, thin roots and insects are their main food and they also eat leaves, sprouts, seeds and fruits. They live gregariously.

Native to China, they receive first grade national protection.

Blue-eared Pheasant

Crossoptilon auritum

Galliformes Phasianidae

Distribution: China's Qinghai, Gansu and Sichuan provinces

Blue-eared Pheasants are 95cm long and they are specific of China. Their dwelling places are in cold areas in high altitude and most live in valleys with rivers or wide and sparse bushes, pine and oak forests. They are gregarious pheasants and live in pairs only during breeding. At night, they perch on trees together.

They receive second grade national protection.

Golden Pheasant

Chrysolophus pictus

Galliformes Phasianidae

Distribution: central China

Golden Pheasants are 98cm long and they are one of the most beautiful pheasants. Moving solitarily or in small groups, they dwell on hills with bushes or subtropical broad-leaves forests. They are good runners and occasionally they perch on trees.

They receive second grade national protection.

White-necked Long-tailed Pheasant
Syrmaticus ellioti
Galliformes Phasianidae
Distribution: southeastern China

White-necked Long-tailed Pheasants are 81cm long and they dwell in the dense bushes and bamboo of mixed forests. They are easily alerted and move in small groups. They often perch on trees and feed on plants and insects. The males become ferocious and likely to fight each other during the April-June mating season.

They receive first grade national protection.

Chinese Copper Pheasant

Chrysolophus amherstiae

Galliformes Phasianidae

Distribution: southwestern China, northeastern Myanmar

Chinese Copper Pheasants are 150cm long and live in places 2,000-4,000 meters above sea level, being able to endure cold. They often move among the bushes of rocky areas and bamboo forests. They live alone or in pairs. A male and many females can also live together. They live in groups in winter and excel in running. They eat sprouts, seeds and insects, but bamboo shoots are their favorite food. The males are famed for their bright plumages.

They receive second grade national protection.

Silver Pheasant
Lophura nycthemera
Galliformes Phasianidae
Distribution: southern China, Southeast Asia

Silver Pheasants are 94-110cm long and they dwell in the mountainous areas with forests, especially liking to move among bamboo forests and bushes. They perch on tree branches at night and run quickly once alerted. Fruits, seeds and insects are their main food, but they also eat leaves, sprouts and flower petals. In April, they enter the mating period and the males often fight each other at that time. One male can mate with several females.

They receive second grade national protection.

Cinereous Vulture

Aegypius monachus

Falconiformes Accipitridae

Distribution: western and northern China, South Europe, middle Asia and northern India

    Cinereous Vultures are 100cm long and they live in plateau and mountainous regions at an altitude of 2,000-4,500 meters. They are good flyers and have a sharp sense of smell and good eyesight. They often fly high in the sky to search for food. In small groups, or together with Himalayan Griffons, they peck the corpse laid out on the ground. Occasionally, they also attack animals.

    They receive second grade national protection.

Himalayan Griffon

Gyps himalayensis

Falconiformes Accipitridae

Distribution: China's Tibetan Plateau, western and central China's high-altitude areas, Middle Asia to the Himalayas

Himalayan Griffons are 120cm long and they are common species of large birds of preys that eat rotten corpse. They often fly high in the sky in small groups or perch on rocky cliffs. They build nests in the crevice of cliffs. The males and females build up their nest, hatch and look after the nestling together.

They receive first grade national protection.

Northern Goshawk

Accipiter gentilis

Falconiformes Accipitridae

Distribution: scattered all over China except Tibet, North America, Eurasia, North Africa

Northern Goshawks are 56cm long. They are forest dwellers. Their wings are wide and round, and they are able to quickly turn, twist and coil. They feed on pigeons, birds and small mammals. Living alone, they catch their prey by gliding directly towards them. Sometimes, they hide among the branches to wait for prey.

They receive second grade national protection.

Golden Eagle

Aquila chrysaetos

Falconiformes Accipitridae

Distribution: northeastern, central and western China, North America, Europe, North Africa

Golden Eagles are 85cm long and they dwell on rugged and dry plains, cliffs and broad fields. Being ferocious birds and capable of flying quickly, the Golden Eagles build their nests on the crown of trees 15-18 meters above the ground or on steep cliffs.

They receive first grade national protection.

Besra Sparrow Hawk
Accipiter virgatus
Falconiformes Accipitridae
Distribution: eastern and southern China, Southeast Asia, India

    Besra Sparrow Hawks are 33cm long and they hide in the forests to catch reptiles and birds.

    They receive second grade national protection.

Northern Hobby

Falco subbuteo

Falconiformes Falconidae

  Distribution: breeds in Eurasia and northwestern Africa, migrates to the South in winter

Northern Hobbies are 30-37cm long. They fly quickly enough to catch swallows. They have sharp eyesight and are able to hunt for big insects such as bats and dragonflies in dim light. They catch their prey with their claws and swallow them while flying.

They receive second grade national protection.

Asian Barred Owlet

Glaucidium cuculoides

Strigiformes Strigidae

Distribution: southern China, Himalayas, northeastern India and Southeast Asia

Asian Barred Owlets are 24cm long and dwell in plains and hills. They usually move at night, although occasionally in the daytime. Insects are their main food, but they also eat mice, other birds and reptiles. They build their nest in tree holes or occupy other birds' nests.

They receive second grade national protection.

Brown Wood Owl ▶

Strix leptogrammica

Strigiformes Strigidae

Distribution: areas south of China's Zhejiang Province, India to Southeast Asia

Brown Wood Owls are 50cm long. Being nocturnal, they shrink their bodies and feathers in the shape of a part of rotten wood with their eyes half closed when they are disturbed in daytime. They catch mice and insects after dusk. They build their nest in the holes of tall trees and are resident birds in subtropical mountainous forests.

They receive second grade national protection.

Imperial Eagle

Aquila heliaca

Falconiformes Accipitridae

Distribution: China, northwestern India

Imperial Eagles are 75cm long and dwell in mountainous forests, grassland and marshland. They tend to fly alone, or perch on a tree, rock or mountainous areas to wait and catch mice, rabbits and pheasants, or feed on the corpses of these animals. They sometimes even rob food from other big birds.

They receive first grade national protection.

Great Pied Hornbill

Buceros bicornis

Coraciiformes Bucerotidae

Distribution: southwestern area of China's Yunnan Province and southeastern Tibet, India, Southeast Asia, Malaysian Peninsula and Sumatra

Great Pied Hornbills are 125cm long and only live in tropical low-lying evergreen forests. Wild berries are its main food. It has a special habit of building a nest. The female, which is hatching the eggs, stays inside a tree hole. The male covers the hole with mud and only leaves a small area for him to pass food to the female. After the nestling hatches, the female breaks out of the nest. Then, the couple cover the tree hole with mud again and feed their nestlings until the latter in turn break out of the nest.

They receive first grade national protection.

Wedge-tailed Green Pigeon

Treron sphenura

Columbiformes Columbidae

Distribution: southwestern China, Himalayas, Java

    Wedge-tailed Green Pigeons are 33cm long and they dwell in mountainous areas with plenty of oaks, bays and Chinese photinia. They move in flocks in the valleys and mountainous broad-leaved forest. Berries are their main food. They move with other migrating nocturnal birds and are photo-tactic.

    They receive second grade national protection.

Rufous-necked Hornbill

Aceros nipalensis

Coraciiformes Bucerotidae

Distribution: southern areas of China's Yunnan Province and southeastern Tibet, Himalayas between Nepal and Indochina peninsula

Rufous-necked Hornbills are 117cm long. They live in evergreen forests at an altitude of 600-1,800 meters. They live alone, in pairs or in small groups. Fruits are their main food.

They receive second grade national protection.

Long-tailed Broadbill

Psarisomus dalhousiae

Passeriformes Eurylaimidae

Distribution: southern China, Himalayas, Southeast Asia to Borneo

The Long-tailed Broadbill is 25cm long. Its whole body is covered with green feathers, making it quite beautiful. Living in tropical evergreen broad-leaves forests at an altitude of 700-1,500 meters, they gregariously search for food in wet bushes or small trees. Seeds, nuts, banyan fruits and insects are their main diet, and they can catch insects while flying. They often look for food among tree branches covered with moss. Their nests look like pears and hang on tree branches.

They receive second grade national protection.

Blue-winged Pitta

Pitta moluccensis

Passeriformes Pittidae

Distribution: eastern and southeastern Asia

Blue-winged Pittas are 20cm long, and, having beautiful feathers, are widely appreciated by bird keepers. Living in dense bushes of tropical and subtropical forests, they perch and chirp away on the top of the trees. But they mainly hop along the ground to search for food. They breed in northern areas and migrate south in winter.

They receive second grade national protection.

Hill Myna
Gracula religiosa
Passeriformes Sturnidae
Distribution: southern areas of China's Guangxi Zhuang Autonomous Region and Yunnan Province, Hainan Island, India, Southeast Asia to Great Sunda Islands

Hill Mynas are 29cm long and they live in tropical rainforests and forests. They often search for fruits and berries on the top of trees in small groups. They also catch for insects, flying ants and suck honey from flowers. On the ground, they can only hop clumsily. Since they are able to imitate a person's language, they are very popular.

They receive second grade national protection.

Mustached Parakeet
Psittacula alexandri
Psittaciformes Psittacidae
Distribution: southern China, India, Southeast Asia to the Great Sunda Islands

Mustached Parakeets are 34cm long and they live in the mountainous evergreen broadleaf forests. Sometimes they also haunt bamboo forests or sugarcane fields. They flock together and in autumn, a large group can be made up of several hundreds. They feed on seeds, fruits, honey and sugarcane.

They receive second grade national protection.

Red-billed Leiothrix

Leiothrix lutea

Passeriformes Timaliidae

Distribution: southern China, Himalayas to northern Vietnam

Red-billed Leiothrix are 15.5cm long and they flock together in the bushes and bamboo groves of evergreen broadleaf forests and mixed evergreen deciduous forests. Many Red-billed Leiothrix often perch on the same branch. Being omnivorous, they feed on insects, fruits and seeds. Red-billed Leiothrix are delicate and have bright feathers. Their chirp is clear and touching.

They receive second grade national protection.

AMPHIBIANS

Amphibians evolved from the fish. They are the earliest vertebrates moving from water to land. Their bodies are covered with skin, but have no scales or fur. They are protozoa, evolving to reptiles, birds and mammals. Amphibians are important for studying the evolution of animals. Except for the Polar Regions, there are about 3,000 species of amphibians scattered around the world. China has 274 species, 175 of them native.

Indian Bullfrog

Rana tigrina

Anura Ranidae

Distribution: China's eastern, central, southern and southwestern provinces

The body length of the Indian Bullfrog is 10cm or above. They have coarse skins. Their backs are yellow green brown and have irregular stripes. They have white bellies. Various sizes of spots dot their forelegs and hind legs. The males have a pair of vocal sacs on the outside of their throats. They live in the open wild, water fields and ponds near mountains. Insects, earthworms, spiders and other small frogs are their main food.

They receive second grade national protection.

Chinese Giant Salamander

Andrias davidianus

Caudata Cryptobranchidae

Distribution: China's northern, central, southern and southwestern provinces

The body length of the Chinese Giant Salamander is more than one meter and they are native to China. They are also the largest amphibians. Since their voices are similar to a baby's cry, they are called "baby fish". They have a round, flat head and big mouth. They have no eyelids and their eyesight is poor. The body is flat and pleated skin covers its side. The limbs are short and flat. They have five fingers for forelimbs and four toes for hind limbs, all of which have little webs. Their bodies are smooth and covered with mucus. The backs of the Chinese Giant Salamander have the colors of mixed black and brown red and the colors of their bellies are lighter. They live in clean brooks in mountainous areas and often hide in the stone crevices of brooks. Their caves are under water. Small fish, frogs and mollusks are their food.

They receive second grade national protection.

REPTILES

Reptiles evolved from the amphibians. They are more adapted to life on land and their bodies are covered with horny scales. Their temperature varies and they are not homoiothermic animals. They breed by producing eggs. There are about 6,000 species of reptiles in the world except in the Antarctic. China has 387 species, 133 of them native.

Asian Water Monitor

Varanus salvator

Lacertiformes Varanidae

Distribution: China's Guangdong Province, Guangxi Zhuang Autonomous Region, Yunnan Province and Hainan Province

The Asian Water Monitor is one of the largest lizards in China. It is nearly 2 meters long and its tail occupies three-fifths of the entire length. Small scales cover the body. It has a long head and mouth. Its limbs are strong and its back is black mixed with yellow stripes. Its belly is light yellow or gray, decorated with black stripes. Living near mountainous brooks, it is good at swimming and is also able to climb trees. It feeds on small mammals, fish and frogs. It settles down in caves or tree holes on riverbanks.

They receive first grade national protection.

Chinese Alligator

Alligator sinensis

Crocodiliformes Alligatoridae

Distribution: bordering areas of China's Anhui, Zhejiang and Jiangsu provinces

The adult Chinese Alligator is about 2 meters long, smaller than many other alligators in the world. It digs caves on the banks of rivers, lakes and ponds as its living place. Being ferocious, it feeds on mice, birds, amphibian reptiles and fish. The Chinese Alligator is a cold-blooded animal and becomes active only when the temperature is above 25 Celsius Degrees. If the temperature of the surrounding environment is low, it lies on riverbanks and enjoys the sunshine with its big mouth open. The Chinese Alligator hibernates in winter. The Chinese Alligator is very timid and quickly escapes into water when alerted; it seldom attacks and hurts human beings.

They receive first grade national protection. ▼

Chinese Crocodilian Lizard

Shinisaurus crocodilurus

Lacertiformes Shinisauridae

Distribution: Dayao Mountain in China's Guangxi Zhuang Autonomous Region

Chinese Crocodilian Lizards are 3-3.6cm long and their tails are longer than their bodies. Their bodies are similar to both crocodile and lizards, hence the name. They have coarse skins and their heads are square, with clear edges on both sides of the head. Their limbs are short and small. They have sharp and curved claws on the front of their fingers and toes. Living in mountainous brooks, they move at dawn and dusk. In daytime, they sleep on twigs and jump into water immediately when alerted. They hibernate from November to the following March. Insects are their main food and they also eat tadpoles, frogs and small fish.

They receive first grade national protection.

Indian Python

Python molurus bivittatus

Serpentiformes Boidae

Distribution: China's Yunnan, Guizhou, Fujian, Guangdong and Hainan provinces and Guangxi Zhuang Autonomous Region

The Indian Python is China's largest nonpoisonous snake. Its body is 6-7 meters long and there is a clear dividing line between its head and neck. The Indian Python is a primitive snake. Living in tropical and subtropical forests, it is good at climbing and also able to live in water. Being a nocturnal animal, it searches for vertebrates as its food. Sometimes, it is able to swallow calves weighing dozens of kilograms. When catching food, they entangle their prey until they are suffocated to death.

They receive first grade national protection.

Shell Turtle

Eretmochelys imbricata

Testudoformes Cheloniidae

Distribution: spread in the tropical sea from Pacific to Indian Ocean

 Shell Turtles are large turtles. The body length is 1 meter and they weigh about 50kg. Each Shell Turtle has 13 shells. Being ferocious animals living in warm sea, they feed on fish, crustacean, mollusks and seaweed.

 They receive second grade national protection.

Impressed Tortoise

Manouria impressa

Testudoformes Testudinidae

Distribution: China's Hainan Island and Xishuangbanna in Yunnan Province

 The adult Impressed Tortoise is 30cm long and 27cm wide. The colors of the back are yellow brown while their sides are black brown. They have strong and round limbs. Dwelling in mountainous forests, they feed on leaves and fruits of plants. They rest by day and move around at dawn and dusk.

 They receive second grade national protection.

Green Sea Turtle

Chelonia mydas

Testudoformes Cheloniidae

Distribution: spread in warm water of the Pacific Ocean, Indian Ocean and Atlantic Ocean

   They are large turtles. Their bodies are more than one meter long and weigh over 100 kilograms. Their back shells are brown yellow and their head, neck and limbs cannot shrink into the shell. Living in the sea, they feed on fish, crustacean, mollusks and seaweed.The females can produce eggs several times a year.

   They receive second grade national protection.

Distribution of Some of China's Rare Wild Animals

❶ Golden Monkey
❷ Chinese River Dolphin
❸ Yak
❹ Black Muntjac
❺ Tibetan Antelope
❻ Red-crowned Crane
❼ Chinese Alligator

❷ Yunnan Snub-nose Monkey
❺ South China Tigher
❽ Thorold's Deer; White-lipped Deer
⓫ Takin
⓮ Crested Ibis
⓱ Brown-eared Pheasant
⓴ Chinese Crocodilian Lizard

❸ Giant Panda; Bamboo Bear
❻ Kiang
❾ Tufted Deer
⓬ Takin
⓯ Black-necked Crane
⓲ White-necked Long-tailed Pheasant

图书在版编目（CIP）数据

中国珍奇野生动物 / 张词祖 主编． −北京：外文出版社，2002.7
（中华风物）

ISBN 7-119-03060-4

Ⅰ. 中...　Ⅱ. 张...　Ⅲ. 野生动物:珍奇动物－中国－图集　Ⅳ. Q95-64

中国版本图书馆 CIP 数据核字（2002）第 026218 号

"中华风物"编辑委员会

顾　　问：蔡名照　赵常谦　黄友义　刘质彬
主　　编：肖晓明
编　　委：肖晓明　李振国　田　辉　呼宝珉
　　　　　房永明　胡开敏　崔黎丽　兰佩瑾

责任编辑：杨春燕
英文翻译：李　京
英文审定：贺　军
摄　　影：张词祖
内文设计：蔡　荣
封面设计：蔡　荣

中国珍奇野生动物

张词祖　主编

© 外文出版社
外文出版社出版
（中国北京百万庄大街 24 号）
邮政编码：100037
外文出版社网页：http://www.flp.com.cn
外文出版社电子邮件地址：info@flp.com.cn
sales@flp.com.cn
外文出版社照排中心制作
天时印刷(深圳)有限公司印刷
中国国际图书贸易总公司发行
（中国北京车公庄西路 35 号）
北京邮政信箱第 399 号　邮政编码 100044
2002 年(24 开)第 1 版
2002 年第 1 版第 1 次印刷
（英文）
ISBN 7-119-03060-4/J·1591(外)
05800(平)
85-E-536P